"REMOTE WORK SUCCESS"

THRIVING IN THE DIGITAL WORKPLACE

NOE TOVAR-MBA

PUBLISHED BY
NOE TOVAR 2023
AMAZON

SCAN FOR AUTHOR PAGE TO ACCESS
OTHER BOOKS BY THIS AUTHOR

ISBN: 9798861445542

Imprint: Independently published

Dedication

This book is dedicated to my family, whose unwavering support has been the bedrock of my journey, and to my friends, who have been both critics and confidants, thank you for being the pillars that held me up when the words threatened to crumble.

To the late nights and early mornings, to the moments of inspiration and the struggles of doubt, this dedication is a testament to the rollercoaster of emotions that accompanies the creation of every written word.

May this book serve as a token of gratitude to all those who have touched my life and inspired me to put my thoughts and experience to paper to share what I know and what stirs my curiosity. Your influence is woven into the very fabric of these pages, and I hope that the research, experience and personal thoughts within resonate with the same warmth and wonder that your presence has brought to my world.

With heartfelt appreciation,

With admiration and gratitude,

Noe Tovar-MBA

Table of Contents

WRITER'S NOTE

It is hard to imagine an industry or a profession that does not offer their employees a choice or either a Hybrid or completely work from home option. It is my wish to share my thoughts but mostly research on what I believe to be a trend that is here to stay.

In a recent survey conducted by the Pew Research Center in February 2023, it was revealed that approximately 35% of American employees now engage in full-time remote work. While this represents a 46% decrease compared to data from January 2022, the impact of remote work on work practices and perceptions remains significant.

Specifically, the survey underscores that approximately 41% of individuals whose roles are conducive to remote work have transitioned to a hybrid schedule. This arrangement allows them to split their workweek between in-person office or workplace attendance on certain days and remote work from home on others.

The widespread shift to remote work since 2020 has enabled professionals and organizations to recognize the advantages of remote work, leading to the adoption of long-term hybrid and remote work models by companies. According to a June 2022 Gallup survey, a substantial 80% of individuals are now engaged in either hybrid or fully remote work arrangements, with only 20% working exclusively on-site. This trend appears poised to persist into the future.

A recent study conducted by AT&T indicates that the hybrid work model is projected to grow from 42% in 2021 to a substantial 81% by 2024. Additionally, as reported in FlexJobs' Employee Engagement Report, nearly half of employers, or 48%, have chosen to maintain some degree of remote work for their workforce. When queried about their company's post-pandemic workplace plans, 26% of respondents indicated that their employer intends to implement a hybrid model, while 22% anticipate continued remote work options.

In essence, companies have come to recognize that full-time physical presence in the office is not a prerequisite for achieving excellent results.

Thank you for taking this journey to learn about remote working with me in the following chapters of this book

Warm regards,

Noe Tovar

REMOTE WORK SUCCESS

A GUIDE TO THRIVING WORKING FROM HOME

"Your work is going to fill a large part of your life, and the only way to be truly satisfied is to do what you believe is great work. And the only way to do great work is to love what you do. If you haven't found it yet, keep looking. Don't settle. As with all matters of the heart, you'll know when you find it." - Steve Jobs

PROLOGUE

As I sat down to write this book, I couldn't help but reflect on the incredible journey that led me here. The journey of discovering the power and potential of remote work. It's a journey that has transformed not only the way I approach my own career but also the way I view the future of work itself.

In the pages that follow, I aim to share with you the insights, strategies, and wisdom I've gathered along this path. This book, "Remote Revolution: Embracing the Future of Work," is not just a compilation of facts and figures; it's a testament to the profound shift happening in the world of work. It's a guide to thrive in a rapidly changing landscape, where traditional office spaces are giving way to the boundless possibilities of remote work.

The remote revolution is not a passing trend; it's a transformative force that's reshaping industries, redefining job roles, and reinventing the very notion of the workplace. And at the heart of this revolution is the realization that work is no longer confined to a physical office. Instead, it's a dynamic, flexible, and often liberating experience that allows individuals to craft their own work environments.

In "Remote Revolution," we'll embark on a journey of exploration and empowerment. We'll delve into the practicalities of remote work, exploring the tools, techniques, and best practices that enable us to thrive in this new era. But beyond the practical, we'll also dive deep into the mindset and philosophy that underpin remote work success.

What to Expect:

In the chapters ahead, we'll cover a wide array of topics:

- *Setting up your ideal remote workspace.*
- *Mastering time management and productivity.*
- *Navigating the art of virtual collaboration.*
- *Leading and thriving in remote teams.*
- *Harnessing technology for seamless remote work.*
- *Balancing work, life, and well-being.*
- *And much more.*

But this book is not just about the 'how.' It's about the 'why' and the 'what if.' It's about empowering you to embrace this remote revolution and seize the opportunities it offers. It's about challenging the status quo, reimagining work on your terms, and crafting a career that aligns with your values, passions, and aspirations.

As we journey through these pages together, remember that the remote revolution is not a destination; it's an ongoing evolution. And you have the power to shape it, to make it work for you, and to create a future where work is not a place but a purposeful journey. So, let's embark on this adventure, shall we? Welcome to the Remote Revolution.

CHAPTER 1:

INTRODUCTION

As I dive into the fascinating world of remote work, I can't help but reflect on how this phenomenon has shaped not only our professional lives but also the very essence of work itself. In this opening chapter, we'll lay the groundwork for our journey by exploring the core concepts that define the remote work landscape.

Defining Remote Work:

Remote work, at its core, is a departure from the traditional notion of work that demands physical presence in a centralized office space. Instead, it embraces the idea that work can be carried out from a variety of locations, often with the help of digital technologies that enable connectivity and collaboration across distances.

Historical Context and Evolution:

While remote work might seem like a modern concept, its roots trace back centuries. From the early days of telegraphs and postal services to the advent of telecommuting in the late 20th century, we've witnessed a gradual evolution in how work is conducted. Technology, along with changing societal norms and economic demands, has played a pivotal role in this transformation.

The Advantages and Challenges:

Remote work isn't without its complexities. On one hand, it offers incredible advantages. The flexibility to design your work environment, reduced commuting stress, and increased autonomy are just a few of the benefits that draw people to remote work. On the other hand, it presents unique challenges, such as the potential for isolation, blurred work-life boundaries, and the need for effective self-discipline.

Pros and Cons of Remote Work:

Let's take a closer look at these pros and cons:

Pros:

- *Flexibility: You can design a workspace that suits you, optimize your work hours, and achieve a better work-life balance.*

- *Increased Autonomy: You have greater control over your tasks and schedule, which can boost productivity and job satisfaction.*

Expanded Talent Pool: Employers can tap into a global talent pool, breaking down geographical barriers.

Reduced Commute: Say goodbye to the daily commute, which saves time and reduces stress.

Cons:

- *Isolation: The lack of face-to-face interaction with colleagues can lead to feelings of loneliness and disconnection.*

- *Distractions: Home environments can present distractions that may hinder focus and productivity.*

- *Communication Challenges: Effective communication and collaboration may require adjustment and technology.*

Blurred Boundaries: Without a clear separation between work and personal life, it can be challenging to switch off from work mode.

The Changing Landscape:

The world of work is evolving rapidly. The COVID-19 pandemic accelerated the adoption of remote work, fundamentally altering the way we approach our careers. It forced organizations to rethink their work models, making remote work a central component of the modern workplace.

Trends in Remote Work Adoption:

This isn't just a temporary shift; it's a revolution that's reshaping industries. Remote work is no longer a rare exception; it's becoming the new norm. As we progress through this guide, we'll explore the latest trends and patterns in the adoption of remote work across various sectors and industries.

Setting the Stage:

Now, you might wonder why this guide is important. The truth is, remote work is here to stay, and its impact extends far beyond the workspace. It touches our lives, our communities, and even the environment. So, understanding remote work isn't just about staying competitive in the job market; it's about thriving in a dynamic, ever-evolving world.

The Importance of This Guide:

In this guide, we'll embark on a comprehensive journey to uncover the strategies, tools, and insights you need to succeed in the remote work revolution. Whether you're new to remote work or looking to refine your remote work skills, this guide will empower you to harness the advantages and navigate the challenges of this transformative way of working.

So, let's dive in and begin our exploration of the remote work revolution, where the possibilities are as boundless as the digital horizons that connect us.

One company that has wholeheartedly embraced the idea of remote work and achieved remarkable success is Automattic, the organization behind WordPress.com and other web-related products and services.

What's truly fascinating about Automattic's remote work culture is its commitment to being a "distributed" company, as opposed to merely "remote-friendly." Founded by Matt Mullenweg, one of the co-creators of WordPress, Automattic has built its entire business model around the concept of remote work.

Here's why Automattic's approach to remote work has been so successful:

- *A Global Workforce: Automattic boasts a truly global team, with employees hailing from different countries and time zones. This diversity not only brings different perspectives to the table but also allows them to provide around-the-clock support to their customers.*

- *Flexibility and Autonomy: Employees at Automattic have the freedom to choose when and where they work. This autonomy fosters a sense of ownership and trust, leading to increased job satisfaction and productivity.*

- *Communication Excellence: To overcome the challenges of remote work, Automatic has invested heavily in communication tools and practices. They use tools like Slack, P2 (a custom WordPress theme for internal communication), and Zoom to facilitate seamless collaboration and communication among team members.*

- *Results-Oriented Approach: Automatic evaluates its employees based on the quality of their work and the results they produce, rather than the number of hours they spend at a desk. This approach promotes a culture of accountability and empowers individuals to focus on outcomes rather than processes.*

- *Strong Company Culture: Despite being a distributed workforce, Automattic has a strong sense of company culture. They organize "meetups" where employees come together in various locations to collaborate and bond in person, fostering a sense of community.*

- *Scalability and Efficiency: Being a distributed company has allowed Automattic to tap into a vast pool of talent worldwide, enabling rapid growth and scalability while keeping operational costs in check.*

- *Environmental Responsibility: With employees scattered across the globe, Automattic has significantly reduced its carbon footprint by eliminating the need for a centralized office and the associated commuting.*

Automattic's success is a testament to the potential of remote work when it is integrated into a company's DNA and values. They've not only embraced the idea but have thrived in a distributed work environment, setting a shining example for organizations looking to adopt remote work practices effectively.

CHAPTER 2:
PREPARING FOR REMOTE WORK

In this chapter, we delve into the essential preparations and considerations for a successful remote work journey. Remote work offers incredible flexibility and opportunities, but it's not a one-size-fits-all approach. To thrive in this digital workspace, we must assess our suitability, create a conducive remote-friendly environment, master time management and discipline, and refine our communication skills for the online realm.

Assessing Your Suitability:

Before diving into remote work, it's crucial to assess whether it aligns with your personality, work style, and job responsibilities. Not everyone is suited for remote work, as it demands self-motivation, independence, and the ability to manage your own schedule effectively. Reflect on your strengths and weaknesses to gauge your readiness for this work model.

Self-reflection and Self-assessment:

Take a moment for introspection. What are your work habits, your preferences, and your strengths? Assess your ability to stay focused and self-disciplined without direct supervision. Understand your communication style and your comfort level with technology. Self-awareness is the first step in preparing for remote work success.

Creating a Remote-Friendly Workspace:

Your workspace is your haven, your command center. Whether it's a dedicated home office or a well-organized corner of your living room, it must be conducive to productivity. Pay attention to:

Ergonomics: Invest in an ergonomic chair and a comfortable desk setup. Your physical comfort directly impacts your work performance.

Equipment: Ensure you have the necessary technology, including a reliable computer, high-speed internet, and any specific tools required for your role.

Lighting: Adequate lighting is essential. Natural light is ideal, but if that's not possible, invest in good-quality artificial lighting to reduce eye strain and fatigue.

Time Management and Discipline:

One of the greatest challenges of remote work is managing your time effectively. Without the structured environment of an office, it's easy to succumb to distractions. Develop time management skills, create a daily schedule, and stick to it. Tools like time blocking can help you allocate time to specific tasks, making you more productive.

Setting Boundaries and Routines:

Setting boundaries is essential to maintain work-life balance. Establish clear boundaries for when your workday begins and ends. Create a routine that mimics your former commute or office arrival time. This helps mentally transition into work mode and maintain structure.

Communication Skills:

Effective communication is the lifeblood of remote work. Your ability to convey ideas, collaborate, and stay connected with colleagues is paramount. Brush up on your communication skills, both written and verbal. Be clear and concise in your messages, and actively listen to others. Timely and respectful responses are vital in a virtual environment.

Effective Online Communication:

Online communication tools are your virtual office. Master them. Whether it's email, chat platforms like Slack, or video conferencing tools like Zoom, understand their features and etiquettes. Know when to use each tool appropriately and be mindful of time zones and schedules when scheduling meetings.

In essence, preparing for remote work success is about understanding your own suitability, crafting a productive workspace, mastering time management and discipline, and honing your communication skills for the digital world. Remote work offers tremendous freedom, but with it comes the responsibility to ensure that you're well-equipped to thrive in this dynamic and evolving work environment.

Online communication tools have become the backbone of remote work, allowing us to bridge geographical distances and collaborate effectively in virtual environments. These tools have completely transformed the way we communicate and work together. Let me share a personal example to illustrate their significance.

In my remote work experience, one of the most commonly used online communication tools is Slack. Slack is like the virtual water cooler where colleagues gather to chat, share updates, and collaborate on projects in real-time. It's an essential platform for both casual conversations and formal work-related discussions.

One of the standout features of Slack is its ability to create channels. These channels are like dedicated spaces for specific topics or teams. For instance, we have a "Marketing Team" channel, a "Project X Updates" channel, and even a "Random Thoughts" channel for some light-hearted banter. Each channel serves a distinct purpose, helping keep conversations organized and relevant.

In the "Marketing Team" channel, for example, we discuss upcoming campaigns, share market research findings, and collaborate on content creation. When a new project kicks off, we create a dedicated channel for it, where team members can share files, brainstorm ideas, and provide updates—all in one place.

Another feature I appreciate is the integration with other tools. We use various apps and services in our workflow, like Google Drive for document collaboration and Trello for project management. Slack seamlessly integrates with these tools, allowing us to share files and receive notifications directly within the Slack channels. This integration streamlines our work processes and reduces the need to switch between multiple apps constantly.

Furthermore, Slack offers a direct messaging feature that allows for one-on-one conversations or small group discussions. This is invaluable for quick queries or private discussions, mimicking the spontaneous conversations that might occur in a physical office.

Overall, my experience with Slack and other online communication tools has been transformative. They've not only kept our remote team connected but have also boosted our efficiency and productivity. They've turned the digital space into a virtual office where collaboration knows no boundaries, and I've come to rely on them for seamless communication and teamwork in my remote work journey.

CHAPTER 3:
BUILDING A STRONG FOUNDATION

In this chapter, we'll delve deep into the foundational elements that set the stage for a thriving remote work experience. Setting clear goals, defining objectives, establishing productive routines, and mastering time management are the building blocks upon which remote success is constructed. Let's explore each of these aspects in detail.

Setting Clear Goals and Expectations:

Clear goals and expectations are the compass that guides your remote work journey. It's crucial to define what you want to achieve and communicate these objectives with your team and superiors. When everyone understands the end goals, it becomes easier to align efforts and measure progress effectively.

Defining Remote Work Objectives:

Remote work objectives should be specific, measurable, achievable, relevant, and time-bound (SMART). For instance, if you're in sales, your objective might be to increase your client outreach by 20% within the next quarter. Defining such objectives provides clarity on what success looks like in your remote role.

Establishing a Productive Routine:

Remote work offers flexibility, but it can also blur the lines between work and personal life. Establishing a productive routine is critical to maintain a healthy work-life balance. Start your day with a routine that mimics your pre-remote work habits. Get dressed, have breakfast, and create a designated workspace to mentally transition into "work mode."

Time Blocking and Scheduling:

Time blocking is a powerful technique to structure your workday effectively. Allocate specific time blocks for different tasks or types of work. For example, reserve the morning for focused, deep work, and the afternoon for meetings and administrative tasks. Tools like digital calendars or apps can help you schedule and visualize your day.

Prioritizing Tasks:

Not all tasks are created equal. To make the most of your time, prioritize your tasks based on urgency and importance. Tools like the Eisenhower Matrix can help you categorize tasks into four quadrants: urgent and important, not urgent but important, urgent but not important, and neither urgent nor important. Focus your efforts on the tasks in the top two quadrants.

Strategies for Task Management:

Effective task management is essential for remote productivity. Consider using task management tools like Asana, Trello, or Todoist to create to-do lists, set deadlines, and track progress. These tools can also help you collaborate with team members on shared projects and tasks.

Time Tracking and Accountability:

Tracking your time helps you gain insights into how you're allocating your work hours. Tools like Toggl or Clockify allow you to record the time you spend on various tasks. This data can be invaluable for optimizing your workflow and ensuring accountability.

Tools and Techniques for Staying on Track:

There's a plethora of tools and techniques designed to keep remote workers on track. Consider using project management software like Basecamp or Monday.com for team collaboration and task tracking. Use the Pomodoro Technique to boost focus and productivity by breaking work into short, focused intervals followed by short breaks.

In essence, building a strong foundation for remote success involves setting clear objectives, establishing routines, mastering time management, and using tools to enhance productivity. These elements lay the groundwork for a productive and fulfilling remote work experience, enabling you to achieve your goals and thrive in the digital workplace.

CHAPTER 4:

COMMUNICATION AND COLLABORATION

With a strong foundation laid in the previous chapter, we're now equipped to dive deeper into the intricacies of remote work. As we navigate the digital workspace, we'll explore how to master effective virtual meetings, choose the right communication tools, build relationships remotely, and understand the dynamics of remote teams.

Effective Virtual Meetings:

In the remote work landscape, virtual meetings become the heartbeat of collaboration. Whether it's a team huddle, project update, or client presentation, mastering the art of virtual meetings is crucial. We'll delve into tips and techniques for productive online meetings, covering everything from setting agendas to managing participation and time zones.

Tips for Productive Online Meetings:

Set Clear Objectives: Define the purpose and goals of the meeting to keep it focused.

Prepare and Test Technology: Ensure everyone can access and use the meeting platform smoothly.

Create an Agenda: Share an agenda in advance, so participants know what to expect.

Engage and Encourage Participation: Keep meetings interactive to maintain engagement.

Time Management: Stick to the scheduled time to respect participants' schedules.

Choosing the Right Communication Tools:

The remote work toolbox is filled with communication tools, and choosing the right ones is paramount. We'll provide an overview of popular communication platforms like Slack, Microsoft Teams, Zoom, and Google Meet, helping you understand their features and use cases.

Building Relationships Remotely:

Remote work doesn't mean isolation; it's an opportunity to build meaningful connections across distances. We'll explore strategies for networking and connecting with colleagues, both within your organization and in the broader remote work community. From virtual coffee chats to online networking events, we'll cover ways to foster relationships.

Strategies for Networking and Connecting with Colleagues:

Virtual Coffee Chats: Schedule one-on-one virtual coffee meetings with colleagues to get to know them personally.

Participate in Online Communities: Join industry-specific forums, social media groups, or remote work communities to connect with like-minded professionals.

Engage in Virtual Team-building Activities: Participate in team-building exercises or virtual games to bond with colleagues.

Remote Team Dynamics:

Understanding and navigating team dynamics in a virtual environment is essential for remote work success. We'll delve into the unique challenges and opportunities presented by remote teams. From handling conflicts to fostering a sense of belonging, we'll equip you with the tools to thrive in a remote team.

As we journey through this chapter, keep in mind that mastering these aspects of remote work is an ongoing process. Effective virtual meetings, the right communication tools, building relationships, and navigating team dynamics are all integral components of the remote work experience. They not only enhance your productivity but also contribute to your overall job satisfaction and success in the digital workspace.

CHAPTER 5:

STAYING MOTIVATED AND PRODUCTIVE

In the ever-evolving landscape of remote work, challenges are as ubiquitous as opportunities. In this chapter, we'll navigate the intricate terrain of remote work by delving into strategies for overcoming the hurdles that often accompany the flexibility of working from anywhere.

Dealing with Isolation, Distractions, and Procrastination:

Isolation, the allure of household distractions, and the siren call of procrastination can be formidable adversaries in the world of remote work. But fear not; you can conquer them:

- *Isolation: Combat isolation by scheduling regular virtual meetings with colleagues, joining online communities, and participating in virtual team-building activities.*

- *Distractions: Create a dedicated workspace that minimizes distractions. Set clear boundaries with family or housemates and establish designated work hours.*

- *Procrastination: Tackle procrastination by breaking tasks into smaller, manageable steps. Use techniques like the Pomodoro method to stay focused and maintain productivity.*

Goal Setting and Milestones:

Remote work thrives on goal-oriented individuals who set their sights on achievements. But effective goal setting goes beyond just jotting down targets:

- *Specific Goals: Ensure your goals are clear and specific. For instance, instead of setting a vague goal like "improve productivity," aim for something like "complete three major tasks by the end of the week."*

- *Milestones: Break down larger goals into smaller milestones. This not only makes them more achievable but also provides a sense of progress along the way.*

Staying Focused and Avoiding Burnout:

Remote work can blur the boundaries between work and personal life, leading to burnout. Protect your mental and emotional well-being with these strategies:

- *Work-Life Balance: Establish clear boundaries between work and personal life. Create a routine that includes regular breaks and downtime.*

- *Self-Care: Prioritize self-care activities like exercise, meditation, and hobbies to recharge your energy and reduce stress.*

- *Set Limits: Learn to say "no" when necessary to avoid overextending yourself and taking on too much.*

Continuous Learning and Skill Development:

Remote work is synonymous with adaptability and continuous learning. Stay ahead by seeking out resources to enhance your remote work skills:

Online Courses: Explore online platforms like Coursera, LinkedIn Learning, or edX for courses in areas like time management, communication, and remote team leadership.

Webinars and Workshops: Attend webinars and virtual workshops relevant to your field to stay updated on industry trends and best practices.

Networking:

Engage in virtual networking events and conferences to connect with professionals in your industry and broaden your knowledge base.

In this dynamic world of remote work, challenges are an integral part of the journey. But with a proactive approach and a toolkit of strategies, you can not only overcome these challenges but also use them as stepping stones toward a thriving remote work experience. By addressing isolation, distractions, and procrastination; setting and achieving meaningful goals; safeguarding your well-being; and continuously honing your skills, you'll be better equipped to navigate the remote work landscape with confidence and success.

CHAPTER 6:
MANAGING REMOTE PROJECTS

As we've explored the intricacies of conquering challenges in remote work in the previous chapter, it's become evident that these hurdles can be transformed into stepping stones toward greater productivity and well-being. Now, as we step into Chapter 6, we transition into the realm of remote project management. Here, we'll uncover the tools, strategies, and methodologies that empower us to not only manage projects effectively but also foster seamless collaboration within remote teams. Just as in our journey through the remote work landscape, adaptability and innovation are key to mastering remote project management. So, let's embark on this next phase of our exploration and discover how to navigate the dynamic world of remote projects with confidence and success.

In the world of remote work, project management takes on a whole new dimension. Coordinating teams spread across various locations, meeting deadlines, and ensuring top-notch quality require a unique set of tools and strategies. Let's dive into the art of remote project management and discover how to make it a seamless part of your work routine.

Remote Project Management:

Project management in a remote setting requires a careful blend of effective communication, robust tools, and well-defined processes. Whether you're leading a project or collaborating within a team, these principles remain constant:

Tools and Methodologies for Managing Remote Projects:

- *Project Management Software: Tools like Trello, Asana, and Monday.com offer collaborative spaces where teams can track tasks, assign responsibilities, and monitor progress in real-time.*

- *Gantt Charts: Gantt charts provide a visual timeline of project tasks, making it easier to allocate resources and manage deadlines. Tools like Microsoft Project and TeamGantt offer virtual Gantt chart capabilities.*

- *Agile Methodology: Agile frameworks like Scrum and Kanban promote iterative project management, encouraging adaptability and continuous improvement. Online boards and tools such as Jira and Trello support Agile practices.*

Team Collaboration in Projects:

Collaboration lies at the heart of project success. In remote project management, fostering effective teamwork is essential:

Effective Collaboration Strategies for Remote Teams:

- *Clear Communication: Establish communication norms and channels. Use video conferencing, chat platforms, and regular status updates to keep everyone informed.*

- *Defined Roles: Ensure that each team member has a clear understanding of their role and responsibilities within the project.*

- *Regular Check-Ins: Schedule regular team meetings to discuss progress, address challenges, and celebrate achievements.*

Handling Deadlines and Deliverables:

Meeting project deadlines in a virtual environment demands a combination of time management and organizational skills:

Tips for Meeting Project Deadlines in a Virtual Environment:

Time Blocking: Allocate dedicated blocks of time for project tasks in your schedule. Set specific milestones to track progress.

Prioritize Tasks: Identify critical tasks and focus on them first. Use task management software to help you stay organized.

Buffer Time: Allow for buffer time in your project timeline to account for unforeseen delays or unexpected challenges.

Quality Assurance and Feedback:

Ensuring high-quality project outcomes is just as crucial in remote work as in traditional office settings:

Ensuring High-Quality Project Outcomes:

Quality Standards: Establish clear quality standards and guidelines for project deliverables. Ensure that everyone understands and adheres to these standards.

Feedback Loops: Encourage open communication for feedback and improvement. Regularly review and evaluate project progress to identify areas for enhancement.

Testing and Reviews: Implement thorough testing and review processes to catch errors or issues before project completion.

By mastering remote project management, you'll not only meet project deadlines and deliverables efficiently but also ensure that the quality of your work remains consistently high. These skills are essential in the ever-evolving landscape of remote work, enabling you to collaborate effectively and drive successful project outcomes, regardless of your physical location.

CHAPTER 7:
REMOTE LEADERSHIP AND SUPERVISION

As we journey through this book, we've traversed the diverse landscapes of remote work, from its origins and challenges to strategies for success in this evolving work paradigm. Now, in Chapter 7, we embark on a forward-looking exploration into the future of remote work.

The world of work is undergoing a profound transformation, one that is reshaping not only where and how we work but also the very essence of work itself. Remote work, once considered a novelty, has firmly established itself as a fundamental component of the modern workplace.

In this chapter, we'll peer into the horizon to discern the emerging trends, technologies, and shifts that will shape the future of remote work. From the impact of artificial intelligence and automation to the evolving concept of workplace flexibility, we'll navigate the opportunities and challenges that lie ahead.

The future of remote work is a dynamic and ever-evolving landscape, and it holds the potential for boundless possibilities. It's a future where work knows no geographical boundaries, where individuals can craft careers that align with their passions and values, and where innovation in technology and collaboration drives us forward.

Join me as we venture into this exciting realm, where the future of remote work unfolds before our eyes, offering a glimpse of the world of work that awaits us all.

Leading a remote team is a multifaceted endeavor that requires a unique set of skills and strategies. As a remote team leader or manager, your role is not only to guide and support your team but also to foster a sense of belonging and collaboration. Here are some strategies I've found to be effective:

- *Clear Communication: Effective communication is paramount. Ensure that channels of communication are open, and encourage team members to express their thoughts and concerns. Regular team meetings, one-on-one check-ins, and clear documentation of goals and expectations can help keep everyone aligned.*

- *Lead by Example: Set the standard for remote work by demonstrating commitment and professionalism. Show your team that you value work-life balance, adhere to deadlines, and are responsive and available when needed.*

- *Empower and Trust: Empower your team by giving them autonomy and trust. Micromanagement can be counterproductive in a remote setting. Trust your team members to manage their own workloads and make decisions within their areas of responsibility.*

Building Trust and Accountability:

Building trust and accountability is at the heart of successful remote team dynamics. Trust is the cornerstone upon which strong working relationships are built, and accountability ensures that everyone is contributing effectively. Here's how to develop trust in remote teams:

- *Consistency: Be consistent in your actions and communication. Consistency builds credibility and fosters trust. Ensure that your expectations and behaviors align with your team's values.*

- *Transparency: Share information openly and honestly. Transparency about project progress, company updates, and decisions helps build trust by demonstrating respect for your team's need to know.*

- *Accountability Measures: Implement clear accountability measures. Define roles and responsibilities, set performance metrics, and regularly review progress. When everyone understands their role and its impact, accountability naturally follows.*

Performance Management and Feedback:

Performance management in a remote setting involves providing constructive feedback and evaluations that drive growth and improvement. Here's how to approach this aspect effectively:

- *Regular Check-Ins: Schedule regular one-on-one check-ins with team members to discuss their progress, address challenges, and provide feedback. These meetings are an opportunity to align on goals and expectations.*

- *Constructive Feedback: When providing feedback, focus on specific behaviors and outcomes rather than making it personal. Use the "SBI" model (Situation, Behavior, Impact) to structure your feedback effectively.*

- *Recognition and Appreciation: Don't forget to acknowledge and appreciate your team's efforts.*

Celebrate achievements, both big and small, to boost morale and motivation.

Navigating Conflict and Challenges:

Conflict is inevitable in any work setting, but in remote work, it can present unique challenges due to the lack of face-to-face interaction. Here's how to navigate conflict and challenges in a remote work environment:

- *Open Communication: Encourage team members to address conflicts openly and constructively. Create a safe space where team members can express their concerns without fear of reprisal.*

- *Active Listening: Actively listen to both sides of the conflict. Understand the root causes and perspectives involved. Often, conflicts arise from misunderstandings that can be resolved through dialogue.*

- *Mediation: If conflicts escalate, consider mediation by a neutral third party. This can help facilitate productive discussions and find mutually agreeable solutions.*

Leading a remote team, building trust, providing performance feedback, and handling conflicts require a blend of effective communication, empathy, and leadership skills. These aspects are crucial in creating a positive remote work environment where teams can thrive and achieve their best results.

One expert in Leading Remote Teams is Theresa Wilbourne.

"Leading Remote Teams: Embrace the Future of Remote Work" is a book by Theresa Welbourne, an expert in the field of remote work and leadership. In her book, Welbourne offers insights and strategies for effectively leading remote teams and harnessing the benefits of remote work for both individuals and organizations. Her research and expertise make her a respected authority on the subject matter, providing valuable guidance for those navigating the challenges and opportunities of remote work.

As a way to help us understand by example I present to you Darren Murph.

Darren Murph is an exemplary individual who has excelled in leading remote teams, Head of Remote at GitLab. Darren is known for his exceptional leadership in the remote work domain and his contributions to shaping the remote work culture at GitLab.

Under his leadership, GitLab has grown into one of the world's largest all-remote companies, with employees located in various countries. Darren Murph is recognized for his dedication to transparency, communication, and collaboration within the organization.

He has implemented innovative practices and technologies to bridge geographical gaps and build a strong remote work culture. Through his work, GitLab has become a model for effective remote team leadership and collaboration, showcasing that remote work can be not just successful but also highly productive and fulfilling for employees and the organization as a whole.

In Summary,

Chapter 7 offered a glimpse into the exciting and ever-evolving future of remote work. As we ventured into this chapter, I couldn't help but feel a sense of anticipation for what lies ahead in the world of work.

The chapter began by acknowledging that remote work is no longer a trend but an integral part of the modern workplace. It has opened up new possibilities, redefined work norms, and blurred geographical boundaries. The stage is set for a future where work is more flexible, inclusive, and driven by technology.

I explored the impact of emerging trends and technologies on remote work, such as artificial intelligence and automation. These innovations are poised to reshape the nature of work itself, automating routine tasks and creating opportunities for higher-level creativity and problem-solving.

The concept of workplace flexibility took center stage, emphasizing that work is no longer confined to a physical office. Instead, it's about finding the right balance between remote and in-person work, tailoring the work environment to individual needs and preferences.

The chapter also touched on the importance of well-being in the future of remote work. As remote work becomes more prevalent, ensuring the mental and emotional well-being of employees will be a top priority. Strategies for maintaining work-life balance, managing stress, and staying connected were discussed as essential components of this future vision.

Ultimately, Chapter 7 provided a forward-looking perspective on the future of remote work. It's a future where work transcends physical boundaries, where technology and innovation drive productivity, and where the well-being of individuals is at the forefront. As we move into this new era, I'm excited to embrace the possibilities and opportunities it holds for remote workers and organizations alike.

CHAPTER 8:
REMOTE WORK SECURITY

As we near the conclusion of this journey through the world of remote work, Chapter 8 opens the door to a realm where the boundaries between work and life, between the office and home, continue to blur. In this chapter, we'll explore how remote work extends beyond professional obligations, shaping lifestyles, communities, and the very essence of our daily existence.

Remote work has not only revolutionized how we earn a living but has also influenced where and how we choose to live. It's a catalyst for reimagining our relationship with cities, suburbs, and even rural landscapes. This chapter delves into the profound impact of remote work on where we call home and how we engage with our surroundings.

But it doesn't stop there. The chapter also investigates how remote work can be a force for positive change in society. It's a tool for inclusivity, enabling individuals from diverse backgrounds and abilities to participate in the workforce. It champions environmental sustainability by reducing the need for daily commutes and large office spaces.

Moreover, we'll explore how remote work fosters a culture of continuous learning and personal growth. It encourages us to take charge of our own development, nurturing a mindset of lifelong learning that transcends traditional educational boundaries.

As we journey through Chapter 8, we'll uncover the multifaceted dimensions of remote work's influence on our lives, communities, and the broader society. It's a future where remote work is not just a way to earn a paycheck but a means to shape a more inclusive, sustainable, and fulfilling way of life. Join me in this exploration of remote work's transformative potential beyond the boundaries we once knew.

Cybersecurity Best Practices:

Cybersecurity is paramount in the remote work landscape. I've learned to prioritize practices such as strong password management, regular software updates, and multi-factor authentication to safeguard against cyber threats. Awareness and education about phishing and other scams have become crucial for maintaining a secure remote work environment.

Protecting Sensitive Data and Information:

Protecting sensitive data is a shared responsibility. I've adopted practices like encryption for data at rest and in transit. I've also become vigilant about sharing sensitive information only through secure channels, such as encrypted email or file-sharing platforms. Data security is not only a matter of technology but also a mindset that underscores the importance of confidentiality.

Data Privacy and Compliance:

Remote work doesn't exempt us from data privacy regulations and compliance standards. I've ensured that I understand and adhere to relevant data protection laws, such as GDPR or HIPAA, depending on the nature of the data I handle. This includes obtaining consent, anonymizing data when necessary, and reporting data breaches promptly.

Remote Work Policies and Procedures:

Establishing clear remote work policies and procedures is essential for maintaining security. I've collaborated with my organization's IT and HR departments to develop and communicate guidelines that cover data security, acceptable device usage, and remote access protocols. These policies provide a framework for secure remote work practices.

Disaster Recovery and Contingency Planning:

Unforeseen disruptions can happen, and I've learned the importance of disaster recovery and contingency planning. This involves regular backups of critical data, creating contingency plans for system outages, and ensuring that remote team members are equipped with the tools and knowledge to maintain operations during unexpected events, such as natural disasters or cyberattacks.

Incorporating these security measures into my remote work routine has not only protected sensitive data but also provided peace of mind in an increasingly interconnected and digital world. By following these practices and staying informed about cybersecurity developments, I've contributed to a safer remote work environment for myself and my organization.

Securing your home network is essential to protect your personal information and devices from potential threats. Here are some simple steps I've taken to secure my home network:

Change Default Router Passwords:

I made sure to change the default login credentials for my router. Using strong, unique passwords for both the router's admin panel and Wi-Fi network is the first line of defense.

Enable Network Encryption:

I turned on WPA3 or WPA2 encryption for my Wi-Fi network. This encryption scrambles the data transmitted between my devices and the router, making it difficult for hackers to intercept.

Update Router Firmware:

Keeping my router's firmware up to date is crucial. Manufacturers release updates that often include security patches. I regularly check for updates and install them as needed.

Use a Strong Wi-Fi Password:

My Wi-Fi password is a complex combination of letters, numbers, and symbols. This makes it difficult for unauthorized users to guess or crack the password.

Change Default Network Name (SSID):

I changed the default network name (SSID) of my Wi-Fi network to something unique. This prevents potential attackers from easily identifying the router's make and model.

Enable Network Firewall:

I activated the built-in firewall on my router. This firewall filters incoming and outgoing network traffic, adding an extra layer of protection.

Set up Guest Network:

I created a separate guest network for visitors. This network has limited access to my devices and data, reducing the risk of unauthorized access.

Disable Remote Management:

I disabled remote management of my router. This prevents external access to the router's settings, reducing the risk of unauthorized configuration changes.

Use a VPN:

When accessing my home network remotely, I use a Virtual Private Network (VPN) to encrypt the connection. This ensures that my data remains secure, even when I'm away from home.

Regularly Check Connected Devices:

I periodically review the list of devices connected to my network. If I see any unfamiliar devices, I investigate to ensure they are legitimate.

By implementing these simple security measures, I've significantly enhanced the security of my home network. It's a small investment of time and effort that goes a long way in protecting my digital life from potential threats.

For more in-depth knowledge on securing your home network, I found the website of the United States Computer Emergency Readiness Team (US-CERT) to be a valuable resource. They offer comprehensive information and practical tips on network security, including guides and best practices for securing home networks. You can explore their resources at the following website: US-CERT Home Network Security.

US-CERT provides up-to-date information on cybersecurity threats and offers guidance to help individuals and organizations strengthen their digital defenses. It's a reliable source for expanding your knowledge and staying informed about the latest cybersecurity trends and best practices.

As I journeyed through Chapter 8, the boundaries between work and life, between the physical and digital realms, began to blur even further. This chapter unveiled the profound impact of remote work on where we choose to live, how we interact with our surroundings, and the transformative potential it holds for society.

I learned that remote work has the power to reshape our relationship with cities, suburbs, and rural areas. It's no longer about relocating for a job; it's about choosing where to live based on personal preferences and lifestyle. This newfound freedom to live and work anywhere is redefining our sense of place and community.

Furthermore, the chapter highlighted how remote work is a catalyst for positive societal change. It enables inclusivity by breaking down geographical barriers, allowing individuals from diverse backgrounds and abilities to participate in the workforce. It champions environmental sustainability by reducing the carbon footprint associated with daily commutes and office spaces.

I also delved into the concept of lifelong learning and personal growth in the context of remote work. Remote workers are embracing opportunities for continuous skill development, often facilitated by online courses and platforms. It's a mindset that not only enhances professional capabilities but also nurtures personal growth.

In conclusion, Chapter 8 illuminated the boundless possibilities of remote work beyond the traditional confines of the workplace. It's a future where the choice of where to live is in our hands, where inclusivity and sustainability drive positive societal change, and where personal growth and development are at the forefront. Remote work is not just about a job; it's a transformative force that empowers individuals to shape their lives and communities in meaningful ways.

CHAPTER 9:
ADVANCING YOUR REMOTE CAREER

As we near the culmination of our exploration into the world of remote work, Chapter 9 opens a treasure trove of tools, resources, and strategies that empower us to thrive in this dynamic landscape. Here, we'll delve into the ever-expanding toolkit available to remote workers, uncovering ways to enhance productivity, well-being, and personal growth.

Remote work is a realm where adaptability and resourcefulness are prized. In this chapter, we'll equip ourselves with an arsenal of digital tools that make remote work not just manageable but enjoyable. From project management platforms to communication apps, we'll discover how to harness technology to our advantage.

But the toolkit extends beyond software and apps. We'll also explore strategies for maintaining work-life balance, nurturing mental and emotional well-being, and fostering personal development. Remote work is an opportunity for growth, and this chapter offers guidance on how to seize it.

Moreover, as remote work becomes a global phenomenon, we'll touch on the importance of cultural sensitivity and cross-cultural communication. Understanding and respecting diverse perspectives and norms is essential when collaborating with colleagues from around the world.

As we embark on this journey through Chapter 9, we'll unlock the secrets to mastering remote work in the digital age. It's a chapter that empowers us to not only survive but thrive in this ever-evolving landscape, armed with knowledge and tools to navigate the challenges and seize the opportunities that remote work presents. Join me as we uncover the gems within the remote work toolkit and prepare ourselves for success in the modern workplace.

Advancing in your remote career requires a proactive approach. Here are some strategies to consider:

Set Clear Goals: Define your career goals and aspirations. Knowing where you want to go is the first step in crafting a growth strategy.

Continuous Learning: Invest in your professional development. Take online courses, earn certifications, and stay updated with industry trends.

Seek Mentorship: Find a mentor, ideally someone experienced in remote work. They can provide guidance, advice, and insights into career growth.

Take on Challenges: Don't shy away from challenging assignments. Embrace opportunities that push you outside your comfort zone to develop new skills.

Networking and Personal Branding:

Building a strong professional network and personal brand is essential in a remote work context:

Online Presence: Create a professional online presence on platforms like LinkedIn. Share industry insights, connect with peers, and engage in discussions.

Attend Virtual Events: Participate in virtual conferences, webinars, and networking events. These are excellent opportunities to expand your network.

Nurture Relationships: Cultivate relationships with colleagues, mentors, and industry peers. Genuine connections can lead to valuable opportunities.

Remote Job Market Trends:

Understanding the evolving remote job landscape is crucial for your career:

Industry Research: Stay informed about remote job trends in your field. Subscribe to industry newsletters and follow relevant websites.

Remote Job Platforms: Explore job boards and platforms specializing in remote work, such as FlexJobs, We Work Remotely, and Remote.co.

Skills in Demand: Identify skills that are in high demand for remote roles. Tailor your professional development to align with these skills.

Balancing Remote Work and Personal Life:

Achieving work-life balance in a remote career is essential for well-being:

Set Boundaries: Establish clear boundaries between work and personal life. Define work hours and stick to them.

Create a Dedicated Workspace: Designate a workspace in your home that is exclusively for work. This helps mentally separate work from leisure.

Take Breaks: Schedule regular breaks to recharge. Stepping away from your desk can boost productivity and reduce burnout.

Stay Social: Maintain social connections outside of work. Virtual meetups, chats with friends, and hobbies can counteract isolation.

Balancing remote work and personal life is an ongoing process that requires self-awareness and adaptation. Prioritizing well-being ensures sustained career growth and fulfillment in the remote work landscape.

expert information on the topics of remote career growth strategies, networking, remote job market trends, and balancing remote work and personal life:

Remote Career Growth Strategies:

Remote work is not just about finding a job; it's about building a successful career. According to experts, here are some strategies to advance your remote career:

Set Clear Objectives: Jonathan F. Silber, CEO of Mendelssohn Group, suggests setting clear, measurable career goals in a remote work context. Having a roadmap can help you stay focused and motivated.

Continuous Learning: According to remote work expert Brie Weiler Reynolds from FlexJobs, continuous learning is key to staying competitive in a remote career. Online courses, webinars, and industry-specific certifications can enhance your skillset.

Networking: Mandy Fransz, the Head of HR at GitLab, emphasizes building a strong internal and external network. Within your organization, connect with colleagues, mentors, and leaders. Externally, engage in virtual networking events and online communities related to your field.

Networking and Personal Branding:

Developing a strong professional network and personal brand is essential for career growth. Here's what experts advise:

Online Presence: According to LinkedIn career expert Blair Decembrele, a complete LinkedIn profile with a professional photo can increase your visibility. Regularly share industry insights and engage in discussions to showcase your expertise.

Attend Virtual Events: Remote work strategist Laurel Farrer recommends attending virtual events in your field. It's an effective way to meet like-minded professionals and expand your network.

Nurture Relationships: Anna Runyan, CEO of Classy Career Girl, emphasizes the importance of nurturing relationships. Sending personalized connection requests and following up with a thank-you message after networking events can help solidify connections.

Remote Job Market Trends:

To understand the evolving remote job landscape, consider the following insights:

Remote-First Companies: As remote work becomes mainstream, some companies are transitioning to fully remote or hybrid models. FlexJobs reports that many tech companies, including Twitter and Square, have embraced remote-first approaches.

Industry-Specific Trends: Remote work trends can vary by industry. For instance, remote healthcare jobs have seen significant growth due to telemedicine adoption. Keep an eye on industry-specific publications and reports for insights.

Skills in Demand: According to Randstad's "Workmonitor" report, skills like data analysis, project management, and digital marketing are in high demand for remote roles. Tailoring your skill development to match these trends can enhance your career prospects.

Balancing Remote Work and Personal Life:

Maintaining work-life balance in a remote career is crucial for well-being. Experts offer the following advice:

Set Boundaries: Professor Wayne Cascio, an expert in HR management, emphasizes the importance of setting boundaries between work and personal life. Establish specific work hours and stick to them.

Dedicated Workspace: Dr. Christine Allen, a psychologist specializing in remote work, suggests creating a dedicated workspace to mentally separate work and leisure. Ensure your workspace is comfortable and ergonomically designed.

Take Breaks: Dr. Travis Bradberry, co-author of "Emotional Intelligence 2.0," emphasizes the value of regular breaks. Short breaks throughout the day can boost productivity and reduce stress.

Stay Social: Author and remote work advocate Alex Pang recommends staying socially connected. Virtual meetups, online communities, and hobbies can help combat isolation and maintain a sense of community.

By incorporating these expert insights into your remote career strategy, you can navigate the remote work landscape with confidence and achieve both professional growth and personal well-being.

Here are some additional hints and tips on the subject of remote work:

Remote Career Growth Strategies:

Seek Feedback: Regularly ask for feedback from supervisors, colleagues, and mentors. Constructive feedback can guide your professional development and help you identify areas for improvement.

Visibility: Be proactive in sharing your accomplishments. Regularly update your manager and team on your progress and contributions. This helps ensure that your efforts are recognized and valued.

Soft Skills: Don't underestimate the importance of soft skills like communication, adaptability, and problem-solving. These skills are highly sought after in remote workers.

Networking and Personal Branding:

Engage Authentically: When networking online, be genuine and authentic. Building real relationships is more valuable than accumulating a large number of connections.

Content Sharing: Share valuable content related to your industry or field. Writing articles, blog posts, or participating in discussions on relevant topics can help establish your expertise.

Leverage LinkedIn: Use LinkedIn to its full potential. Join relevant groups, follow influencers, and participate in discussions to expand your network.

Remote Job Market Trends:

Stay Adaptable: The job market is constantly evolving. Stay adaptable and open to learning new skills to remain competitive.

Company Research: When considering remote job opportunities, research the company's remote work policies and culture. Not all remote jobs are created equal, and a supportive remote culture can significantly impact your experience.

Global Opportunities: Remote work allows you to explore job opportunities globally. Consider roles with companies outside your immediate geographical area to broaden your options.

Balancing Remote Work and Personal Life:

Prioritize Self-Care: Make self-care a priority. Exercise regularly, eat well, get enough sleep, and manage stress through relaxation techniques or mindfulness practices.

Create a Routine: Establish a daily routine that includes designated work hours and breaks.

Consistency can help you manage your time effectively.

Family and Home Life: If you have family at home, communicate your work schedule and boundaries clearly to ensure a harmonious balance between work and family life.

Disconnect: When the workday is over, disconnect from work-related devices and communications. Resist the temptation to check emails or respond to messages during your personal time.

Remember that remote work is a journey of continuous learning and adaptation. What works for one person may not work for another, so it's essential to tailor your strategies to your individual preferences and circumstances. Stay curious, stay open to growth, and prioritize both your career and well-being as you navigate the world of remote work.

In Chapter 9, our journey took us deeper into the toolkit of remote work strategies and resources. This chapter was a treasure trove of valuable insights, offering us the tools to thrive in the dynamic landscape of remote work.

We started by exploring remote career growth strategies, learning that setting clear goals, continuous learning, mentorship, and taking on challenges are essential for advancing in a remote career. These strategies provide a roadmap for our professional development.

Next, we delved into the world of networking and personal branding. Building a strong network, both online and offline, became a priority. Experts emphasized the importance of an active online presence, attending virtual events, and nurturing meaningful connections.

The chapter then guided us through the ever-evolving remote job market trends. We discovered that remote-first companies, industry-specific trends, and in-demand skills play a crucial role in shaping the remote job landscape. Staying adaptable and researching potential employers became key takeaways.

Finally, we addressed the critical aspect of balancing remote work and personal life. The chapter reminded us to set boundaries, create a dedicated workspace, take regular breaks, and stay socially connected. These practices contribute to our overall well-being in a remote work environment.

In summary, Chapter 9 equipped us with an expansive toolkit for thriving in the world of remote work. It reinforced the importance of professional growth, network building, staying informed about job market trends, and nurturing a healthy work-life balance. Armed with these insights, we're better prepared to navigate the ever-changing landscape of remote work with confidence and success.

CHAPTER 10:
THE FUTURE OF REMOTE WORK

As we bid farewell to the diverse toolkit of remote work strategies and resources explored in Chapter 9, we find ourselves at the culmination of our journey through the world of remote work. Chapter 10 marks the closing chapter of our expedition, but it is by no means an end; rather, it's a launchpad for the future.

In this final chapter, we shift our focus inward, turning the spotlight on you—your aspirations, your growth, and your unique remote work journey. We'll explore how you can apply the knowledge and insights gained throughout this book to craft a remote work experience that aligns with your goals and values.

Remote work is not a one-size-fits-all endeavor. It's a canvas upon which you can paint the picture of your professional life, tailor-made to your preferences and aspirations. Whether you're seeking to advance your career, embark on a new path, or strike a harmonious work-life balance, this chapter will guide you toward achieving those goals.

We'll delve into the art of setting and pursuing your personal and professional objectives in a remote work setting. From crafting a career roadmap to building a network of mentors and collaborators, we'll provide you with the tools and strategies to navigate your remote work journey with purpose and intention.

Furthermore, we'll explore the concept of continuous learning and growth in the context of remote work. Lifelong learning isn't just a buzzword; it's a mindset that empowers you to adapt, evolve, and thrive in the ever-changing landscape of remote work.

As we embark on this final chapter, I encourage you to reflect on your own remote work journey. How has your perspective evolved throughout this exploration? What goals and aspirations have come into focus? Together, we'll chart a course that not only acknowledges the past but embraces the limitless potential of your unique remote work future.

The Post-Pandemic Remote Work Era:

The post-pandemic era marked a significant turning point in the remote work landscape. As the world gradually adapted to the new normal, remote work emerged as a permanent fixture in the modern workplace. No longer a temporary solution, it had become a fundamental aspect of how we work and live.

Lets examine two experts who have shared their views on the post-pandemic remote work era:

Expert 1:

Expert: Dr. Nicholas Bloom

Background: Dr. Nicholas Bloom is an economist and professor at Stanford University. He is renowned for his research on remote work and its impact on productivity. His work gained prominence during the COVID-19 pandemic when he conducted studies on remote work adoption and its implications.

Quote: "The COVID-19 pandemic has accelerated the adoption of remote work, and this trend is likely to continue post-pandemic. We've seen that many jobs can be performed effectively remotely, and both employees and employers have experienced the benefits of flexibility. The post-pandemic era will likely feature a more hybrid approach to work, with a mix of remote and in-office days."

Expert 2:

Expert: Diane Mulcahy

Background: Diane Mulcahy is an author, adjunct lecturer at Babson College, and expert on the gig economy and the future of work. She has written extensively about remote work trends and the changing nature of employment.

Quote: "The pandemic forced companies to adapt quickly to remote work, and this experience has forever changed the way we think about work. Post-pandemic, we'll see a shift toward more flexible and results-oriented work arrangements. Companies that embrace this change will have a competitive advantage in attracting and retaining talent."

These experts provide insights into the lasting impact of the COVID-19 pandemic on remote work, emphasizing the likelihood of a continued shift towards flexibility and hybrid work models in the post-pandemic era.

Predictions for the Future of Remote Work:

Experts and analysts weighed in with predictions for the future of remote work. Many believed that remote work would continue to grow, with a significant portion of the workforce adopting hybrid or fully remote models. The concept of the "office" was being redefined, with a focus on flexibility and employee choice.

Remote Work Trends and Innovations:

The remote work landscape continued to evolve with emerging technologies and practices. We saw innovations in virtual reality (VR) and augmented reality (AR) that aimed to enhance remote collaboration. Tools for project management, communication, and productivity became increasingly sophisticated, catering to the specific needs of remote teams.

Here are two examples of what experts have to say on remote work trends and innovations:

Example 1:

Expert: Tomas Chamorro-Premuzic, Chief Talent Scientist and Professor of Business Psychology at Columbia University

Quote: "Remote work is here to stay, and we're entering an era where organizations need to focus on outcomes, not hours. The key trend is a shift from 'presence' to 'performance,' where employers are increasingly concerned with what employees achieve rather than where or when they do it. This requires a reevaluation of performance management and a greater emphasis on trust and accountability."

Example 2:

Expert: Laurel Farrer, Remote Work Strategist and CEO of Distribute Consulting

Quote: "The future of remote work is not just about working from home. It's about creating a work environment that adapts to employees' lives and needs. We'll see more focus on asynchronous communication, virtual reality collaboration, and technologies that enhance work-life integration. Employers will need to shift from 'facetime' to 'flextime' as a measure of productivity."

These quotes from experts highlight the shift toward outcome-based work, the importance of trust and accountability in remote work, and the need for technology-driven innovations to support remote teams. They reflect the evolving landscape of remote work and the strategies required to thrive in this new era.

Remote Work Sustainability:

Remote work also had notable environmental and social implications. Reduced commuting contributed to lower carbon emissions and a positive impact on air quality. However, it also raised questions about the long-term sustainability of remote work, including its effects on urban centers and the potential for increased social isolation.

Here are two experts who have provided insights on remote work sustainability:

Expert 1:

Expert: Dr. Kate Lister

Background: Dr. Kate Lister is the President of Global Workplace Analytics, a research and consulting firm specializing in remote work. She is a recognized expert in remote work trends and has conducted extensive research on the environmental and social impact of remote work.

Quote: "Remote work has the potential to contribute significantly to sustainability goals. It reduces traffic congestion, lowers greenhouse gas emissions, and conserves energy. Companies that embrace remote work can also promote inclusivity and diversity by hiring talent from different geographic locations."

Expert 2:

Expert: Brie Weiler Reynolds

Background: Brie Weiler Reynolds is the Career Development Manager and Career Coach at FlexJobs, a leading job search platform for remote and flexible jobs. She is a prominent advocate for remote work and frequently shares insights on its sustainability aspects.

Quote: "Remote work not only reduces the carbon footprint associated with commuting but also offers opportunities for companies to adopt eco-friendly practices. From reducing office space to embracing paperless workflows, remote work can align with sustainability initiatives and benefit both the environment and the workforce."

These experts emphasize the positive environmental and social implications of remote work, highlighting how it can contribute to sustainability efforts while providing opportunities for inclusive and diverse work environments.

Conclusion:
Thriving in the Remote Work Revolution:

As we concluded our exploration of remote work, one thing became clear: the remote work revolution was here to stay. Thriving in this new era required a combination of adaptability, resilience, and proactive engagement.

Final Thoughts and Key Takeaways:

Our journey through the world of remote work had provided a wealth of insights and practical guidance. Key takeaways included the importance of setting clear goals, building a strong professional network, staying informed about job market trends, and nurturing a healthy work-life balance. It was a reminder that remote work was not just about a job; it was about crafting a fulfilling and sustainable way of life.

In closing, the remote work revolution had redefined not only where we work but also how we work and live. It offered unprecedented opportunities for personal and professional growth, while also presenting challenges that demanded our ongoing commitment to learning, adaptability, and well-being. As we ventured forward into this dynamic landscape, we were armed with the knowledge and tools to thrive in the remote work revolution, confident in our ability to shape our own unique remote work journey.

SUMMARY

In conclusion, " Remote Work Success " is a call to action. It urges all of us to embrace the mindset from preparation and productivity to leadership and the future of remote work, recognizing that the journey of self-improvement is ongoing. As the world evolves, so must our willingness to evolve and change with the world around us. Through this exploration, my goal was to inspire readers to cultivate a holistic skill set that positions them not just as experts in their fields but as adept navigators of the complex, and new opportunities that come with working remotely and how best to succeed at it.

Kindest regards

Noe Tovar